ANANDIBAI JOSHEE

Celebrating
30 Years of Publishing
in India

Praise for *Anandibai Joshee: A Life in Poems*

'In this act of poetic ventriloquism, Shikha Malaviya draws inspiration from a singular woman—one who walked a solitary path with élan. A spirited speaker emerges from these pages: one who sees a stethoscope as precious jewellery, who realizes that "all hearts sound the same regardless of intentions", and when asked what epoch she would like to live in, is able to answer resolutely, "The Present." This innovative retelling of a remarkable life story is a step towards restoring voice and agency to yet another woman protagonist in history on whom the "Mute" button has too long been pressed.'

—Arundhathi Subramaniam, Author of *Love Without a Story* and *When God is a Traveller*

'I was struck by Shikha Malaviya's interrogation of voice in these poems, the way she deftly conjured this visionary woman from the past and shape-shifted her towards us, reminding us how kaleidoscopic we are as individuals, how connected.'

—Tishani Doshi, Author of *A God at the Door* and *Girls Are Coming Out of the Woods*

'Shikha Malaviya's *Anandibai Joshee: A Life in Poems* brings to the fore an often forgotten figure of migration and power. Joshee (1865-1887), the first Indian woman to enter the United States, has become the poet's daemon—whose deity she honors with devotion. Malaviya's poems illuminate the affective interior of the first Indian woman doctor through immersion into the poet's practice: specificity, tension, and release. These are Joshee's words, just as they are not—a strategy that invites readers to consider the possibility of a South Asian woman's own representation of herself in the Global North; a metaphor for the poet to consider her own inheritance of Joshee's legacy. Based on Joshee's own journals, letters, public records, and photographs, the collage Malaviya uses, shows readers how lyric forms can bend into experimentation and how a complicated life needs poetry to write it. It takes a Dante-like expertise to lead the reader through the chaukat of biography and onto the jhopala of imagination's courtyard. This is a book I will gift to many, many people, as it is, itself, a gift to all of us.'

—Rajiv Mohabir, Author of *Cutlish* and *Antiman: A Hybrid Memoir*

ANANDIBAI JOSHEE

A Life in Poems

Shikha Malaviya

HarperCollins *Publishers* India

First published in India by HarperCollins *Publishers* 2023
4th Floor, Tower A, Building No 10, DLF Cyber City,
DLF Phase II, Gurugram, Haryana – 122002
www.harpercollins.co.in

2 4 6 8 10 9 7 5 3 1

P-ISBN: 978-93-5699-407-2
E-ISBN: 978-93-5699-406-5

Typeset in 11.5/15.2 Minion Pro at
Manipal Technologies Limited, Manipal

Printed and bound at
Thomson Press (India) Ltd

FSC www.fsc.org MIX Paper from responsible sources FSC® C010615

This book is produced from independently certified FSC® paper to ensure responsible forest management.

for Yamuna Gunpatrao Joshee

We give on this page a portrait of Mrs. Anandibai Joshee, a Brahmin lady of high social standing, who has recently produced a sensation in India by breaking away from the fetters of Hindoo thought and customs…Here and there voices have been raised, during the last few years, in behalf of the emancipation of the sex from the tyranny of old ideas and superstition, but no such pronounced action has been taken by anyone as by Mrs. Joshee…Impressed by a conviction that one of the best methods of helping her sex in India would be the promotion of thorough medical knowledge, she resolved to seek a medical education, and on the 7th of April last left Calcutta for Philadelphia, where she will enter the Female College for a thorough course of medical study.

—From *Mrs. Anandibai Joshee, Leader of the Movement for Woman's Emancipation in India,* Frank Leslie's Illustrated Newspaper, 12 March 1883

She looks like a stout, dumpy mulatto girl not especially interesting until her yellow face lights up, and light up it did as soon as she gathered from a helping word of mine, that I was familiar with the customs of her people. I cannot describe the effect. It was magical. She speaks seven languages, of which English, Sanscrit and Mahratta are three. Her English is exquisite. There is hardly a flaw in pronunciation or construction. If I had not known, I should have thought her born in this country.

—Diary entry of Mrs. Caroline Healy Dall. 6 October 1883, Philadelphia, USA

When it is remembered that the Brahmins are forbidden to cross the ocean, to eat food which has not been prepared by Brahmins, or to drink water touched by European hands, and that the violation of these orders involves severe penalties, Mrs. Joshee's heroism becomes strikingly apparent.

—Mrs. Caroline Healy Dall, The Life of Dr. Anandabai Joshee, A Kinswoman of Pandita Ramabai, 1888

A woman who feels an irresistible urge to study medicine so strong as to overcome her natural timidity, or to be willing to take the obloquy and covert, if not open, insults from the world in general, and very often her own family and friends in particular—she will make a better doctor than a stupid lout.

—*Dr. August Gardner,* Frank Leslie's Illustrated Newspaper, 1870

CONTENTS

PREFACE

Dear Reader,

The following historical persona poems are culled from the life and letters of Anandi Gopal Joshee (also spelled as Joshi), known widely as Anandibai, who lived from 1865-1887.

Anandibai was India's first female physician and the first Indian woman to enter the United States in 1883 to pursue an education in medicine. An interest in Anandibai resurfaced around 2017, when her black and white photograph from Drexel College of Medicine's Legacy Center archive went viral on the Internet. Her life story is a compelling one of empowerment and American and Indian allyship—in which Anandibai broke tradition and social conventions by crossing tabooed black waters (kala pani) to pursue an education and career held exclusively by men. Until very recently, Anandibai's story has been told through the lens of her husband being her savior and inspiration. And while he encouraged her, it was often by coercion and violence. By telling Anandibai's story through poems in her own voice, my hope is to not only restore Anandibai's agency and give her story back to her, but to also highlight her inner strength, determination, sharp intellect, and desire to help other women.

But how and why did I write this book?

In 2017, I was researching South Asian history for a long lyric poem I was writing on the racism I had experienced as a child while growing up in Minnesota in the early '80s. In this poem, I wanted to confront a childhood bully with facts and dazzle him, to let him know that my family wasn't the first to have come from India, so that his words, 'go back to where you came from', would ring hollow. It had always been convenient for me to slip into the notion that I was the 'other' and that America wasn't my actual home, because I hadn't seen myself or my history reflected in my surroundings. This led me on a wild goose chase of sorts to find out who was the first woman from India to touch American shores. And suddenly there she was, seated in a sepia-tinted photograph, next to two other women, dressed elegantly in a saree, her Mona Lisa-like glance following me everywhere, her lips curled up in a half-smile, her image radiating such fierce determination that I had to know more. Who was this woman and how did she get to Philadelphia all alone from India in the 19th century and why? How did she break away from that iron grip of tradition where women were largely homebound tending to family and manage to cross kala pani, those black ocean waters that were considered tainted? I was riveted and literally felt a shiver—of acknowledgment and discovery, this validation of knowing that all along there had been others before us. This was how I stumbled upon the extraordinary life of Anandi Gopal Joshee, known more informally as Anandibai, possibly the first Indian (Hindu) woman to have come to the United States. Until very recently, Anandibai's story was limited to her geographic community in India and had been told through the lens of her husband being her advocate and guide. I wondered if I were to tell Anandibai's story through poems in her own voice, what would that mean? How would it change the narrative? Would it give her agency back to her? Would it give South Asian Americans a deeper sense of roots and history? And supposing it did, was I the right person to undertake this task? I was a poet after all, and not a historian.

It is with these hesitations that I began my research and poem-making. And stopped. And started. And stopped. And began again. For four years, Anandibai would simmer in the back of my mind like a pot of dal on the stove. I was intimidated by what I found and what I hadn't. There was a biography written in Marathi, Anandibai's mother tongue, of which I barely knew a few words. There was also a Marathi novel that had been translated into English that captured the time period well, but painted a picture of Anandibai that seemed weak, helpless, and at the whims and mercies of her mercurial husband. It barely mentioned Anandibai's time in the United States. Drexel University's Legacy Center Archives brought me a little closer to the person that was Anandibai. It was here that I came across that iconic photograph of three women from three different countries posing in their native dress—a saree, a kimono, a headdress of coins—gathered in Philadelphia to become doctors and then return home to serve the people of their respective lands. Yes, this photograph echoed exoticism, orientalism and the West's fetishization of the East, and yet it exuded a kind of power that seemed to turn the notion of empire on its head and hint at an allyship and sisterhood that went beyond the church and state. There were more photos of Anandibai, one, a side profile with her signature in both Devanagari and English, and a letter in her long, slanted writing stating why she would be an ideal candidate for medical school, a newspaper clipping celebrating the arrival of the first woman medical student from India, and more. She was becoming more real by the second. And yet every 21st century article on Anandibai I came across espoused the same narrative:

India's first woman doctor. Born in 1865. Married at nine to a widowed man sixteen years older who was zealously progressive. Pregnant at twelve or fourteen, Anandibai loses her child (a son) ten days after giving birth due to lack of medical care. The loss fuels her desire to become a doctor, only there are no medical schools for women in India. Anandibai's husband does everything he can to help her become one, including pleading with American missionaries and possibly converting to Christianity. An American woman in New Jersey hears of Anandibai's plight and offers assistance and Anandibai goes to America, all by herself, despite the protest of her own countrymen and women. Anandibai returns to India as a doctor and is celebrated/hailed for her bravery but dies of tuberculosis before she can practice.

So where was Anandibai in all of this? Trapped between the narrative of the husband as savior and the white wo/man as savior was Anandibai's own voice and it resounded so loudly in my mind and heart. Could no one else hear it?

Two women, a century apart, had heard Anandibai's voice and had tried to capture it in their own ways in English. The first, Mrs. Caroline Healy Dall, a feminist writer and reformer, had met Anandibai (but referred to her as Anandabai) while she was in America and after their first meeting had written in her journal:

> She looks like a stout, dumpy mulatto girl not especially interesting until her yellow face lights up, and light up it did as soon as she gathered from a helping word of mine, that I was familiar with the customs of her people. I cannot describe the effect. It was magical. She speaks seven languages, of which English, Sanscrit and Mahratta are three. Her English is exquisite. There is hardly a flaw in pronunciation or construction. If I had not known, I should have thought her born in this country.

On first reading, I found the journal entry offensive, and it brought back memories of my own childhood where I was told how flawless my English was by white Americans, marveling at how I didn't have an accent. But on closer examination, I was fascinated by the paradoxes within the journal entry. Anandibai had clearly made an impression on Caroline Dall. So much so that she would meet Anandibai several more times and go on to write her biography a year within her passing. While this was a biography of an Indian woman through Western eyes and carried the author's own cultural biases, it incorporated several of Anandibai's letters along with comments from those who were close to her along with a narration of incidents and events. Anandibai's voice was on almost every page through her letters that Dall had collected from various people—a polite and trusting voice, a strong and confident voice, a voice that wasn't afraid to ask questions and share her concerns, a voice that seemed wise beyond her teen years. Best of all, this book, *The Life of Dr. Anandabai Joshee, A Kinswoman of Pandita Ramabai*, written in 1888, was available on the internet, copyright free. I downloaded and printed it twice in four years, between the several stops and starts of this project. This would be my go-to book, as I read it repeatedly, scanning for nuggets of gold, a chance sentence or fact that might reveal a unique facet of Anandibai's personality or experience. Anandibai had visited Tiffany's flagship store in New York. She had also gone to the Barnum & Bailey Circus show with a classmate and had written that she didn't care for it but hadn't specified why. In 1883, Anandibai held an Indian feast for her host family and their friends where the women all dressed up in Anandibai's Indian clothes and sat on the floor eating with their hands. She had even given her host and her daughters Hindu names, and they had remarked they were all turning into "Hindoos." Anandibai's favorite color was white, her favorite place Roselle, New Jersey, and after that, heaven. This she shared in an autograph book at her host's home. It was the smallest details I was looking for and this biography offered them.

The other book I would turn to was published more than a century later, *A Fragmented Feminism: The Life and Letters of Anandibai Joshee* by Meera Kosambi, published in 2020. Meera Kosambi was an Indian sociologist who, like me, was in search of the real Anandibai. Like Anandibai, Kosambi was also from Maharashtra and had access to works and letters in Marathi. She also had access to Dall's biography and drew much from it. Kosambi brought her own critical analysis and questions to the fold, pointing out how Anandibai's husband's ideas of reformation were contradictory and that it was only through the distance of many oceans that Anandibai could come into her own and see that her relationship with him was a difficult one, among other things. With her scholarship, Kosambi connected the dots that Dall never could have. And yet I still felt that something remained to be said. Both these women had captured Anandibai's life; one with a 19th century Western reformer perspective, the other looking more deeply through a 21st century Indian feminist lens, with Anandibai's words to support their respective theses.

Perhaps poetry was that medium which could fill that critical gap between these two important representations of who Anandibai Joshee was, especially if it was poetry imagined in 'her' own voice, from a woman who had inhabited both worlds, a person who had lived both in India and the United States, a woman who, like Anandi, had been torn between traditional expectations and the desire to find out who she was, apart from what others expected her to be. I second-guessed my intentions and yet I continued amassing a pile of facts and images, as the task lay before me of how to translate a woman's life into poems. How much to show, how much to tell, and how much to discern from what was between the lines? How much research was enough?

I looked to others who had undertaken the monumental task of bringing voices of the past to light and drew inspiration from the poems of Tyehimba Jess, who in his extraordinary, polyvocal book, *Olio*, had given voice to unrecorded African American performers in the 18th and 19th century in innovative ways and forms I had never seen before. In searching for women's voices through historical persona poetry, I discovered Dominique Christina's searingly powerful book, *Anarcha Speaks: A History in Poems,* in which she gives voice to Anarcha, a 19th century enslaved black woman on which Dr. J. Marion Sims, the so-called father of modern gynecology, performed horrific experiments in the name of science. Later in my journey, I would come across Honorée Fanonne Jeffers' *The Age of Phillis,* a collection of poems and scholarship that took my breath away in its retelling/imagining of the life of Phillis Wheatley Peters, the very first African American woman who wrote and published a collection of poetry in the 18th century.

As I pondered and processed all of this, the pandemic broke out and raged. My life came to a standstill, while Anandibai's came alive.

In the quietness of a sequestered world, I was able to let the past in. The poems started coming out in a voice that didn't seem like mine—quiet, contemplative, slightly formal, but insistent. To my astonishment, in the span of nine months, I wrote over forty poems, all in the imagined voice of Anandibai. Had she finally come through? The interiority of such undertakings is often part of a solitary journey. But during a pandemic, it felt like living a whole other life despite being grounded.

During the writing of this book, I was acutely aware of the responsibility of portraying caste and the privileges that come with being a high caste Hindu woman in both the 19th and 21st centuries, in my interpreting and retelling of Anandibai's life without being disingenuous to the struggles of Dalit communities. There is no doubt in my mind that Anandibai's being born into a well-respected Brahmin family gave her every advantage, no matter her challenges, and that her status and upbringing informed her day-to-day living and thoughts. Where I have mentioned 'Brahmin' it is because that is how Anandibai identified herself and how others regarded her in the 19th century. It is not to glorify any kind of superiority. I hope, in this regard, I have been able to stay true to Anandibai's voice and story without undermining the reality of Dalit issues and casteism.

I would also like to add that though these poems in the imagined voice of Anandibai Joshee draw from facts in her life, creative interpretations/leaps have been made regarding how Anandibai might have thought, felt and/or responded to different situations.

I am eager to share what I have discovered and written, to let Anandibai's voice and story touch everyone, to reclaim the past in a bid to understand better who we are. I hope you will join me.

If not yourself, whom would you like to be?
"No one."

—Anandibai Joshee, Roselle, New Jersey, 1883, in Theodocia Carpenter's autograph book.

OUTSIDE THE CHAUKAT

Kalyan, Maharashtra, Nineteenth Century

If you want to know what happens in this bustling town by the sea, Kalyan, which in Sanskrit means well-being but whose shores have thrice been plundered by the Mughals, the Portuguese, and the British, despite the shade of a fortress and a long city wall with four gates and eleven towers, whose welfare is erased and renamed *Kallian* and *Cullian*

—ask the men, for they are the ones who wear shoes that take them outside the chaukat. They are the lucky ones, who, donning their turbans, smell the dung of many homes, hear the hum of horses hooves, darken their hands with the ink of newsprint, read the khabar of the day while sitting on a jhopala in the courtyard, dragging a puff from a gurgling hookah

—whereas the women tiptoe softly, their bare soles hardened walking from kitchen-to-cowshed-to well, fingertips charred from stoking the chulha, thoughts spilling over like water from vessels balanced on their heads, of what lies beyond a door frame, that make a splash and then evaporate

NAMING/NÃMKARAN

Aai,
    Is it really true?
        That being named after a river
            is bad luck, a turbulent life?
                Are all women rivers then?
            And tell me the story again
        of how I came to be
    a paisley in your belly
why you named me—
    daughter of the blinding sun
        sister of the lord of death
            tumbling down to earth
                to meet her blue beloved
            how I was born the same day
        as a goddess riverine
    whose holy drops
the priest sprinkled on my forehead
    eleven days after my birth
        introducing me to this world
            whispering into my ear
                Yamuna, Yamuna, Yamuna
            a contract signed in water
        a girl's fate sealed

MIDDLE CHILD

My earliest memories?

The crook of an arm, warm
Aai's saree, soft and worn
scents of sandalwood and soot

my siblings' limbs tangled
as they do kusti with one another
feigning pain amidst laughter

sounds of the jhopala
in the courtyard crick-cracking
drunk on stories of Gods, I swoon

to a gaana, soothing
of burbling green pigeons
—and love seeped in slowly

for this middle child
limbs massaged daily with mustard oil
chin marked with a black spot

to ward off the evil eye

A DIFFERENT KIND OF ARITHMETIC

Before I could count properly on my fingers
Ek don teen char, I learned division

        the haveli halved into two sections
        the mardana and zenana

a different kind of arithmetic—
the louder the men spoke

        the softer the women
        never in the same room

next to each other
unless an auspicious occasion

        children were the exception
        of which I was one

running freely between both
a threat to no one

        like a son I consumed rice
        with extra ghee, tumbling

with my brothers who teasingly
called me malla after I defeated them

repeatedly, I was strong and proud
like our fabled ancestors who served

in courts and wars, whose accounts
lay preserved in scrolls, one whom I met

in a dream, a valiant soldier
who promised great things

were sure to come
Aai tried to beat it out of me

this unladylikeness, this streak of obstinacy
but Babasaheb treated me as one of the boys

indulging my dreams and foibles
his eyes crinkling when I ran to him

each evening under the shade of a giant
Peepal tree, sitting on his lap unloading

the day's thoughts—my fears
and world queries

asking him the difference between
my dolls and idols of Gods

why both lay mute in one's hands
at the mercy of others' inclinations

TO TOUCH THE SKY

1873

The sun's shadow
swept over my face
as I built biceps
drawing water from the well
rope burns on my hands and wrists
and when I complained
there was no time to play
Aai's anger drew welts on my back
her orders a daily refrain—
gather sticks for the chulha
scrub the pakshala
so when I found the jhopala empty
I grabbed its chains as if a horse's reins
pumping my legs furiously
to see how high I could go
braids flying, skirt rippling, sun winking
toes trying to touch the sky
my only witness a green pigeon
whose wings I conspired to steal

THE PROMISE OF WHAT WAS/WHAT WILL BE

1873

They tell me I will have to cast off
dust as my daily apparel
my games and learning adjourned
that I must now join the zenana
and don a saree
that I am pockmarked and plain
that I look older than my age
of eight and who will marry me
their biggest worry
neither fair nor thin
though poor by money
we are rich by reputation
the lands we once owned
sliced off and sold like gaud
till all we have left is
the haveli and grand stories
of ancestors rewarded by peshwas
and who will be lured
by such long gone sweetness
who will unshoulder

the burden that is
unwed girl
who will want
someone like me
so ordinary?

LAGNAACHI BEDI (A SUITABLE MATCH)

'We marry before we know what it is for."
—Anandibai Joshee, in a letter to Mrs. Theodocia Carpenter

1874

Bhatji, the priest, shows up
with scrolls in his satchel
patrikas of prospective grooms
I am never in the room
when they do the guna milan
and how powerful the moon
that determines our alliance
ashtakoot—eight aspects
to see if we match or cross

The stars align—
you are twenty-six and I, not quite nine
no misfortune upon you, though you are widowed
never stripped of color nor sequestered to a harsh life
for it is your good fortune to be born a man
my saubhagya to be a postmaster's second wife
moving place-to-place like a mailed letter
gathering the stamp of bhinn shahere
and how lucky I am you have no demands
no money, no gold, only the promise
to teach me, to make me wise
and when we first meet, you ask my name

Tujhe nav kahe? To gauge my ability
hear my voice, as I stare at my toes
a downward gaze passed
through centuries
when suddenly I lift my head
peer straight into your eyes
and reply, *Majhe nav*
Yamuna Ganpatrao Joshee aahe

HIDE & SEEK

1874

Like phulapakhare
dancing in the summer sun
we play lapachhappi
behind wooden pillars
as the elders nap at noon
my brothers spinning me
round and round and round
in the haveli courtyard
till I become a cloud of dust
and they scatter like marbles
in different directions
shouting 'don't you look'
—and suddenly I'm wearing a nauvari
my nine years cocooned in nine yards
of wedding finery so bright
it almost blinds me, I am all chrysalis
at the mandav as they tell me, 'don't you look,'
bringing up the auspicious antarpat
that separates his face from mine
he, the reluctant groom
I, the unaware bride
both of us hidden from the other
playing lapachhappi together
yoked for seven lives

AN ALTARED STATE

Kalyan, Maharashtra, 1874

We waited
flower garlands in hand
our eyes drooping
as the shubh mahurat passed
banana leaves curled up
all the gaud dried up
our hopes curdled at the mandav
when you didn't show up
everyone whispering
was I not good enough?
—and eccentric is what they said
of you who ran away in search of a widow
to remarry and reform, leaving me forlorn
seven sacred vows unfulfilled

A few weeks later you return
reluctant and resigned
on my birthday where I am all of nine
no widow willing, so you garland a child
a pupil at the altar of your feet
my new name, Anandi, bliss
written in unbroken rice
girl, a synonym for other's whims

Yamuna, now a turmeric stain
that will fade over time
when they lower the antarpat
our eyes finally meet

CONSUMPTION

His tongue
is a sickle
when the words
come out
they cut me
like a handful
of grass
uprooting me
from where I stand
dullard, lazy
incompetent
adjectives he swings
at me again and again
but if this were truly so
he wouldn't press me
between jaws of books
the ink of alphabets
seeping into my skin
staining my blood
this knowledge that
consumes me
as I consume it
he wouldn't hurl
their hard
spines
at me if
he thought
I couldn't
catch
them

CANOPY

> प्रजां च धत्तं द्रविणं च धत्तम्
> *Prajām ch dhattam dravinam ch dhatama*
> bestow upon us progeny and affluence
> — *Rig Veda 8.35.10 - 8.35.12, Translated by Ralph Griffith*

My first blood arrives
a hibiscus shaped splotch
this rude redness that all rejoice
this twisting pain in my groin
an old saree rag between my legs
and within two weeks I find myself
under a canopy, dressed like Goddess Lakshmi
in a nauvari saree, my neck glowing gold
my lap filled with flowers and fruit
a coconut that sloshes when shaken
blessings from Aai and Ajji
all the women in my family already wed
who celebrate the wealth of my womb
as prescribed in the holy Vedas
to invite the gods to plant good seeds
and let it take root, though I know not
how this happens, except that
it takes two, a sthri and purush

BADGE OF BLOOD

1876

The whole house is still. Even the green pigeon in the semal tree outside has stopped burbling and tucks its head under a wing. Night spreads like kohl under weary eyes. He tiptoes into the room and his hot breath is suddenly upon me. Sliding my saree up, he grips my wrists, asserting his rights on the sharir I thought only mine. I start crying. But this is what man and wife do, he tells me, caressing the top of my head, whispering all will be fine. And then the shadow of him covers my own. As green glass bangles break into little shards of grass and my braid comes undone like a river, I become the jhopala in the courtyard rocking back and forth. I think of all the body parts I learnt as a child, how I repeated them over and over to claim them: doke, khanda, ghudga, payachi botey. They teach us so many things, our mothers—to separate the husk from grain, to churn butter from milk, to spell out our new name in a tray of rice the day we are wed, but never do they tell us why the kunku worn after marriage is so red, why we refresh the badge of blood on our foreheads morning after morning.

MARK & MAR

How innocuous this piece of wood
shaped into a likeness of what is useful
table, stool, cooking tools, and fuel
that transform our food, but in his grip
this piece of wood becomes an extension
of his hand that mark & mar my skin
swelling and changing color, pushing
against my blouse so tight, Ajji has to rip
it open with a knife, my husband, whose
consternation is I, with pot and ladle
instead of book and slate, he threatens
to leave me unless I comply
the alphabet dancing before my eyes
                    bruised
black   blue

HOLDER OF THE WORLD

Little one, so fond of ghee
and your mother's touch
every time I rub some on my belly
you move with such gusto, as if a globe
inside me spinning on its axis
striations on my skin taking the shape of rivers
tributaries like the one I was once named after
stretching to hold what he and I have made
and will you have his stubborn pointed chin
my big eyes, hair soft as silk or rough as coconut husk
will your cry be a temple bell or the soft chime of hymns
my hours pass dreaming of who you will be
books gathering dust, as I read
the shifting lines of my body
they all say son, by how you hang low
but I think sun, whose warmth we shall
revolve around, no matter whether girl or boy

THINGS I WISH AA(I) HAD TOLD HER/ SHE HAD TOLD ME

1877

Think of it as a transaction

milk flowing from the breast in a spray, not a trickle

hunger—milk   mouth—nipple

heavy like sacks of guineas

currency of motherhood

even when there's no infant to suckle

milk leaking every two hours

womb shivering after the fact

keeping time with phantom feeds

an empty cradle rocked by sea breeze

LOSS: AN INVOCATION

1877

On the 11th day we were to name you
with careful consideration—
moon sign, birth month, family deity
touching your tongue with honey
that you should speak sweet
a black thread tied around your wrist
to ward off unfriendly glances
but the only ceremony left is mourning
ten days you suckled then went still
and my breasts that leaked every two hours
in memoriam grow hard and cold

This humility that keeps us indoors
is what killed you, my son, what kills our own
shying from a doctor's touch, another man's
we grieve under the shade of our sarees
as men go about their daily business
and through your loss I find purpose
my son with no name birthing a dream
and I volunteer myself to my countrywomen
as I take the oath of Hippocrates
to help and heal, to do no harm, to don
the white coat only men have worn

ANANDI LEARNS ENGLISH

Kolhapur, Maharashtra, 1879

This new language
is like balancing a marble on my tongue
the k in knife—silent, the t in brother—soft
Grandmother says:
why learn the bhasha of the angrez
who don't bathe every day
who eat the flesh of animals like a jungli
and call us heathen instead
because our heads are covered
yet feet bare
But my husband—
he brings me books in awwal Angrezi
He says I must learn it all
their language, their god, their modern ways
anything to help us cross kala pani
to hold their alphabets in my mouth
and swallow before they roll away

MAGNETISM

My husband with his shaved pundit's head and white dhoti
and the Christian missionaries clad in black despite tropical heat
are like two sides of a magnet—opposing forces, yet united by
the same zeal; one pushes to reform the mind, the other
pulls to convert the soul. Do they not know of the center that holds?
None of them ask me what the heart wants, while I hear it loud
like a sambal drum rushing into my ears, beating for the women
of my land, and with a stethoscope I might hear it clearer—
dhad-dhad dhad-dhad, doctor-doctor, of which there are none
from where I come from, of brown hue, clad in colorful sarees
kunku pulsing on their foreheads like red crosses

RIDING WITH MISS MOYSEY

1879, Kolhapur

Because her carriage passes by the post office each morning
and my new shoes give me blisters when I go the distance
because riding with her improves my mind and manners
Miss Moysey's back straight despite the shock of potholes and ditches
a British governess who stayed when her wards returned home
and I, her newest student, high caste Hindoo
most coveted of converts, we sit side by side
on our way to the Government Female School
she in her black hat, I with my saree and stockings
several shades of silence thick between us
each knowing the other as an anomaly, an aberration

SARASWATI IN MY SATCHEL

1880, Bombay Presidency

They proclaim the black age has come, Kali Yuga
because a Hindoo girl walks to school
in leather shoes and stockinged feet
beneath her saree, this unholy union of West and East
because she dares to dream beyond the bhandi-kundi

And all the books I hold in my hands don't stop them
from defiling Saraswati, the Goddess of learning
who resides between words and pages
that I carry in my satchel each morning
as they hurl stones at me and spit on my head
my own people telling me I might as well be dead
so I heed them and become Kali, namesake of this black age
Goddess of death, preying on their ignorance
slaying them each day with my dogged presence

CUTTING THROUGH STONE

As if a rogue kite dancing in the wind

we move from Kalyan to Alibaug to Kolhapur

to Bhuj to Bombay to Serampore

letters on sifaarish by white men

that this brown girl's learning is not mere whim

and the locals visit the post office to gawk

at this postmaster's wife who chooses words

over the hearth, and though lonely we are never alone

their eyes upon us waiting for the fall

my husband's love, tough like the leather of my shoes

books become my closest friends, and water, a companion

following me everywhere—rivers, marshes, the sea

teach me to take the shape of what holds

to be both vessel & its contents within

to be a river that cuts through stone

MY HUSBAND WRITES A LETTER TO REVEREND WILDER

He asks if I am prepared to give my heart to another God
How hard can it be? I'll be your servant and you be
the empress, we'll steal their names, for they've erased ours
he pleads, and their hopes are so great that he will convert
that I should quietly follow, the missionaries whose favour
he requests, a letter addressed to Reverend Wilder
from a Hindoo whose professed passion is
female education, all attempts having fallen short
in his homeland to make his wife a good doctor
and he tells them how I have *a pretty good hand*
in English, that I *can point all the countries on a map*
that though he doesn't *want to live on charity*
he is *very much in need of assistance*, and
though they don't refuse, they mock us
testing our resolve, asking us how strong
the desire, how far can we go
that if we accept Christ, all will be ours
all sins absolved, and is this what it means
to lose oneself, the cost of attaining a dream?
But surely there is a good Samaritan
in this world whose heart is governed
by more than religion, not just ruled by faith
a humanitarian

The following poem is an amalgamation of the letters Anandibai Joshee wrote to Mrs. Theodocia Carpenter between 1880-1883. Words in italics are Anandibai Joshee's words as extracted from her letters, except for the first section and the first line from the second section, which are words extracted from the letter of Theodocia Carpenter.

THE WHOLE UNIVERSE IS A LESSON TO ME: EPISTOLARY EXCHANGES

1880-1883

.I.

Like a cloudburst in this arid land
your letter arrives, despite a new address
some might say fate, but I say miracle
my husband's plea across seven seas
reaching your benevolent eyes
through a magazine that rebukes us
for not accepting as our savior, Christ
yet it stirred your heart, my plight
as an elder sister's would, and so you
address me, *Dear Sister,* opening
doors of *encouragement* and *help*
desirous of serving in any way
with the promise of true friendship
all of us *children of the same God*

.II.

All of us *children of the same God*
from these wise words, dear madam
do I recall, a saying in the Upanishads
Vasudhaiva kutumbakam, this world is one family
and *my gratitude knows no bounds* of that great person
who understands how anxious I am to serve
God and the women of my land, to study medicine
your letter *fills my heart with unspeakable joy*
a growing desire to see where such gems are born
and most fortunate will I be if the almighty affords me
the means to go to America and complete my studies
I have not forsaken my learning and thus *keep up*
fresh memory that in some future day, I may be able
to achieve my object

.III.

To achieve my object
it falls upon England or America to take care of us
though proud and fond of her, I have no hope
of India resuming her motherly duty
to give her daughters nourishment
the more I read and think of your favour
the more I think of you as a real sister
nay, it is more than that, as if entrusted
the care of a child where the mother is absent,
and I am glad to hear America is not so orthodox
if you write to me in my name, there would be
nothing wrong, for my husband's good wishes
allows me the privilege of direct correspondence
I beg your acceptance of my photo lately taken

.IV.

I beg your acceptance of my photo lately taken
you must have seen how *we are fond of many ornaments*
our hands, feet, neck, waist, all adorned to the teeth
The blemish you mention between my nose and lip
is a nose ring, a gold wire upon which are fastened pearls
Though this may appear barbarous to the foreign eye;
to us it is a beauty! Everything changes with the clime
I have no adequate idea about America and her people
I have many things to learn from you, and few to give
in return. So I thank you for all the books and favours
When we began to write, I cared little for letters
but now I see how the daily occurrences of life
which I thought so trifling, may yield instruction
and so I am impatient to see the Western light
dawn(ing) as the harbinger of emancipation

.V.

Dawning as the harbinger of emancipation
I look to the English system in mentioning my husband's name
I cut a lock of my hair in favour of yours, though it is not in our custom
only of those women widowed, and to answer your question of the same
I shudder at the very sound, for the difficulties your widows face
against ours, are *but as a particle against a mountain, undergoing*
mortifications and degradations of all sorts—her head shaved
her red mark wiped, her glass bangles and wreath of black beads
broken, a widow's face first seen in the morning, is but a bad omen
and so she sits in a dark corner as mischievous priests contemplate
her further undoing, never given enough to eat, never allowed to celebrate
no one is more restricted than the brahmin in food and other rituals
prescribing a number of rules. When we eat we use no knives or spoons
our water jug never touched directly by mouths, but poured from above

.VI.

Our water jug never touched directly by mouths, but poured from above
all foods we eat prepared only by brahmins, all water drawn from the well
rice, milk, and ghee, our chief foods, though we are fond of sugar too
the obligations of hindoos are so numerous, that few we accurately fulfil
a hindoo woman toils the whole day ensuring this might happen smoothly
you can imagine the scandal of my education, my desire to go to America
My husband is greatly inclined to send me there for practical knowledge
But does not see his way to it. Suppose I come with the intention of staying?
Can I live in your country as my own, preserving my manner and customs?
I am a vegetarian and do not wish to be Europeanized in food or dress
I wish to carry my custom and manners unless detrimental to my health
I have been ill with something or another. In India, higher class women
are generally very weak. I ascribe the cause to the custom of early marriage
As you complain of the same, there is some wrong in the marriage system

.VII.

As you complain of the same, there is some wrong in the marriage system
No man or woman should depend upon another for necessaries
social degradation will never end till each depends upon herself
I am happy you received the silver filigree I sent you
and the Cutch wildflowers are from the garden I made on your urging
though I had no liking for the care of it, I owe you a great debt
in seeing how all living things flourish on being nurtured
these flowers decorate our altars for worship. Is it so in America as well?
I am sorry, my dear sister, this letter is late, *on account of my serious illness*
which confined me for nearly three weeks. This sickness confirms me
in my desire to study medicine. We Indian women suffer from innumerable
trifling diseases unnoticed till they grow serious. Diseases to which women
are naturally liable are never known to anybody except the sufferers
It is thought indecent to be examined by male doctors, the other sex

.VIII.

It is thought indecent to be examined by male doctors, the other sex
yet we commit ourselves to the doctor's care implicitly, never questioning
his ability and curative powers. Medical advice here is so rare
that thousands upon thousands depend upon nature for a cure
I am much better now, at least free from fever. I am thinking of taking
the medicine, which you so kindly sent as prescribed by your good doctor
which was transmitted to her in sleep. To tell you the truth, I always labor
under inward impressions. I solve many things while sleeping. Whenever
I have anything to learn by heart, I read the passage to be committed
to memory but once in the day, and in sleep, I read it over and over
and repeat it next morning without a mistake. I do not know who
teaches me, but I learn in this way. I would rather be ignorant
and illiterate than to have partial knowledge of everything
anything which cannot be enjoyed by the whole world is bad for me

.IX.

Anything which cannot be enjoyed by the whole world is bad for me
I am required by duty to respect every creed
no religion is bad but its followers and selfish interpreters
our priests are prejudiced and corrupt as those of other religions
I dislike them as a class. If there had been no priesthood
this world would have advanced ten thousand times better
I regard irreligious people as pioneers
In my one year of schooling, I was forced to read the Bible
I have nothing to say against it except the assertion:
"He that believeth shall be saved" and "he who believeth not
Shall be damned." How arbitrary would it be if I were to say
that all you believed was nonsense, and all I believed was
just and proper! My dear friend, I have nothing to despise—
The whole universe is a lesson to me

.X.

The whole universe is a lesson to me
and I share one with you. Every year when the sea goat embarks on its
celestial path, three weeks after the winter solstice, we celebrate
the sun's rays growing longer, the days becoming warmer. We cast off
the bitter and move forward with all sweetness. All mistakes and ill
will from the past year are forgiven. And so, I send you these tila seeds
to celebrate with me. Please accept them and *be friendly with me*
Though these sesame seeds seem tiny, they provide nourishment
during the cold months. We roast them and mix them in jaggery
which we boil and spread on a platter to cool. Then we break them
into small pieces and offer them to our loved ones, saying "Tilagul ghya
ani goad goad bola," wishing all talk sweetly through the year.
Though words are simply words and we are all flesh and blood
calling you Aunt allows me to honor your kindness

.XI.

Calling you Aunt allows me to honor your kindness
I was not sure you would consent, but your willingness augers well
for the future. We are in Calcutta now, reduced in health and strength
from this oppressive heat which takes its toll. My husband comes home
fatigued and falls asleep almost immediately, while I lie awake
The zenana here is so rampant, they are always indoors, behind veils
so when we walk outside together, we are watched and followed
a police sepoy stopped us on the esplanade and asked if we are married
All this makes me feel that this country is not good for us. *At first*
our intention was that we should both start for America, but now
we perceive it to be very expensive. *You can imagine how difficult it is*
for a small purse to pay for two. I am not sorry but think myself happy
I am untyed. Dear Aunt, wherever I cast my glance I see a smooth way
Let me be here, or in any part of the globe, I will get my bread

.XII.

Let me be here, or in any part of the globe, I will get my bread
You have reason to think that a very distant voyage will be hazardous
for a girl of eighteen, but I fear no miseries. Everyone must not ride
on another's shoulders but walk on his own feet. Hundreds urge that
I am liable to go astray and lead an unchaste life, but our ancient Indian
ladies were very wise, brave, courageous, and benevolent, and endurance
was their badge. Let it be my badge also. I am sure nothing will harm me
or if it does, it will be for my own good, I feel that the movements of
my mind is due to the counsels of my husband. What he has taught me
he has so impressed that it will never be effaced. I must launch my fortune
like a ship on the ocean of life. To what shore shall it go, to a fertile bank
or a barren beach? Or will it go to pieces? I promise myself that
if my efforts will be successful, I will return to my native country
I am impatient to see you and to begin to learn what my country needs

WHY I GO TO AMERICA

> *"In 99 cases out of 100, the educated men of this country are opposed to female education and the proper position of women. If they observe the slightest fault, they magnify the grain of mustard-seed into a mountain and try to ruin the character of a woman."*
>
> —Pandita Ramabai Sarasvati's testimony before the Hunter Commission, 1882

February 24, 1883, Serampore

Tucked in the crook of the Hooghly river
a city changes hands and names over centuries
Serampore, a mangling of the name Srirampur
by the British that currently inhabit it
And before that, Frederiknagore, so named
by the Danes after their King, it is here
we reside directly above the post office
where I come under their scrutiny
men who can't bear the thought of
a woman holding a pen filled with ink
the color of kala pani, deep dark waters
no good Hindoo ought to cross
and so they crowd around our home
night and day, throngs of people
with consternation writ on their faces
while letters come and go freely each day
I am trapped in my own home, this postmaster's wife
whose only sin is learning, and they won't relent
until I tell them why I go to America—
for I am that novelty who threatens their purity
a Hindoo woman who dares to leave
a life of domestic drudgery and they all beg

an explanation, a certain satiety
to their many questions, an end
to all their inquiries which I dare to answer
publicly, in the giant hall of Serampore College
built by English missionaries

On that sultry day, the hall fills up with perspiring faces
of townspeople as well as people of the church
of those formally educated and some unlettered
but curious. I look at all of them before begging
pardon for speaking in a language newly acquired
and *stand* in front of them ready *to fail*, my voice
slightly quivering as I tell them in English
I go to America because I wish to study medicine

I implore the ladies present who would know the wants
of our own kind in cases of emergency, where the doctor
is from Europe or America and of the other sex, how we
are not able to say how we truly feel or draw comfort
from their touch, and so *we Indian women derive no benefit*
from those *who are different in manners, customs, and language*
or from our own kind who are men—and *so I volunteer*
to qualify myself as a Hindoo lady doctor

The want of female physicians in India is keenly felt in every quarter
And while there are some means to study here in one's native
—one college and midwifery classes, *the difficulties are many and great*
I do not find fault here with the instructors, yet they *are conservative*
and somewhat *jealous.* T*hat is the characteristic of the male sex*
and *we must put up with this inconvenience until we have*
a class of educated women to relieve these men

I go to America because
to continue to live as a Hindoo
and go to school in any part of India is difficult
my brethren *lay bare their levity*
by making fun of everything
I go alone because *we have not sufficient funds*
and my husband must tend to his aged parents
And shall I not be excommunicated when I return?
I do not fear it. Why should I be cast out
when I have determined to live there
exactly as I do here?
I choose not to look at the dark side
if misfortune befalls me, it must be endured
no man is able to prevent any catastrophe
and is it so bad to go to a foreign country
to enlarge our comprehension, perfect
our knowledge or recover lost arts
Ignorance when voluntary is criminal
I am not disheartened by the thought of failure
We must try. The greater the difficulty
the greater our courage

RIDING THE MERIDIAN

Aboard the City of Calcutta steamship, 1883

Countless creases on these waters
of ships traversing the ocean's face
as the sun plays truant during our voyage
Mrs. X, my companion, draws notches
in the back pages of her bible
of days and nights, feigning prayer
while she eyes my movements, wondering
what is it this Hindoo is reading—
remarking how no book is as worthy
as the black-bound one in her hands

Other passengers look at me unfavorably
as I push bald potatoes and limp vegetables
around my plate, holding a fork and knife gingerly
refusing animal flesh, I ignore their whispers
of how I should be in third class with the ayahs
and yet I wish that were so, for I would find
less pretense there and more color in conversation
no threats of conversion, but in each lip of land
our ship touches I take delight, a different scene
as if from a storybook—Ceylon's tall palms swaying
Egyptian soil gleaming red and England's billowy
clouds like an umbrella over our heads

With the sun's daily revolutions
we move further and further from the equator
at the speed of four to six knots
my saree rippling in salty air
as I inhale the scent of a new world
the seas neither black nor poisonous
but taking shape of the palm that holds it
how does that which has no colour
both bless and stain, all of us, water
and I think of Copernicus who stood
by his convictions, who knew
the true meaning of circumambulation
how it is us that revolves around
what gives us sustenance
and not the other way around

AMERICAN LADY FRIENDS GREET A MAHRATTA WOMAN

A found poem from Anandibai's letter to her husband, Gopalrao

June 1883, Roselle, New Jersey

It is a happy day
they call it a holiday
and the sun so bright
like none they have ever seen
Aunt's lady friends come
embrace and kiss me
they regard my native dress
and manners favorably
caressing the silk of my saree
tapping the kunku on my forehead
as if it has special powers

In the space of a few hours
the visitors who call are many
with golden curls, and fashionable hats
their heads covered out of deference
as my shoulders are with my saree's padar
I sit in a rocking chair with flowers
in my hands. It is past ten and still
they stream in with bouquets
my arms growing heavy
as if holding a sleeping child

I wonder if there is such a thing
as too much love and curiosity?

At last, Aunt shuts the windows
so that no one can see me inside
we have green grass, cool breeze,
hot weather, loving trees
everyone is kind to me
they say I've brought them
Summer, some tropical heat

A MENTAL PHOTOGRAPH

A found poem from Anandibai Joshee's entry in Mrs. Theodocia Carpenter's Autograph book

September 3rd, 1883

I was ravenous
shoving the open mouth
of my mind with morsels
of knowledge held
by my husband's hand
that after crossing two oceans
when I should be asked in the parlor
of my sponsor, a kind American woman
whom I call Mavshi— mother's sister
in my native tongue, but whose love is
like a mother's itself—what my favorite things are
I am truly overcome with joy
no one has ever asked this of me
(Not even I), And so I write
in the album of Mrs. Theodocia Carpenter
of Roselle, New Jersey, ever so carefully
answers that introduce me
to myself

Color—*White.*
Flower—*The Rose.*
Tree—*The Mango.*
Object in Nature—*Mountains.*
Hour—*Sunrise and set.*
Season—*Spring.*
Perfume—*Jasmine.*
Gem—*Diamond.*
Style of beauty—*Perfection of form and manner.*
Name, male and female—*Rama, Tara, Annie, Gopal, Vishnu, and Chrishna.*
Painter—*I love all.*
Musician—*Those who play on the violin and lyre.*
Piece of architecture—*The Taj Mahal.*
Poet—*Pope, Manu, and Kalidasa.*
Poetess—*Muktabai and Janabai.*
Prose author—*Goldsmith, Macaulay, Addison, Shastree Chiploonkar.*
Character in History—*Richard Coeur de Lion.*
Book to take up for an hour—*The Bhagavat-Gita*
What book, not a Bible, would you part with last? *The History of the World.*
What epoch would you prefer to live in? *The Present.*
Where would you prefer to live? *In Roselle now, hereafter in Heaven.*
What is your favorite amusement? *Reading.*
What is your favorite occupation? *Whatever is necessary to the common comfort.*
What is your favorite trait of character? *Sincerity.*
What trait do you most detest? *Dishonesty and infidelity.*
If not yourself, whom would you like to be? *No one.*
What is your idea of happiness? *Faith in God.*
What is your idea of misery? *To follow one's own win.*
What is your bête noire? *Slavery and Dependence.*

What is your ideal pleasure? *To be rewarded for what I do.*
What is your distinguishing characteristic? *I have not yet found out.*
That of your husband? *Benevolence.*
What is the sublimest passion? *Love.*
What are the sweetest words? *Love, charity, truth, and hope.*
What are the saddest ? *Lost, forsaken.*
What is your aim? *To be useful.*
What is your motto? *The Lord will provide.*

IF IT PLEASE GOD

Each time she tells the story
I'm convinced it isn't coincidence
call it fate, nasheeb
aunt's eye falling on the dusty cover
of the Missionary Review
her tooth throbbing in the dentist's office
as she flips through it, till her eyes rest
on my husband's plea
I should, therefore, if it please God
like to take my wife to America
for her being thoroughly educated
our maker surely one and the same
conspiring to shrink oceans and bring us closer
three years later, I say goodbye
to Serampore's dark shores
my new home now Roselle, New Jersey
where hope bursts open like as a rose
giving 'let there be light' new meaning
making history as the first town to be electrified
by Thomas Edison a few months before I arrive
as the first Mahratta woman studying medicine
and I bask in this newly lit town, under the love of
another mother, another land, where I can be myself
desirous of learning, without others' injurious glances
burning bright as a bulb

A PLEA TO MAKE HERSTORY

A found poem culled from a letter written by Anandibai Joshee to Alfred Jones on June 18, 1883, requesting admission in the Woman's Medical College of Pennsylvania.

Dear Sir,

I beg to be allowed to enter the Women's Medical College of PA
upon any terms pecuniarily consistent with my means
please trust that my case is exceptional and peculiar
I am pushing forward as fast as I can
I have learned to read and speak in seven languages
Marathi, Sanscrit, Bengali, Gujarathi, Ganari, Hindoostani, & English
I have read the histories of England, Rome, Greece, and India
I have been through English Grammar and studied through Arithmetic
& though I may not meet in all points the requirements for entering college,
this determination which has brung me to your country against opposition
of my friends & caste, ought to go a long way

CASTE AWAY

Roselle, New Jersey, 1883

It is a different life here, surely, in America
Aunt's home seems more wood than stone
the cold of their beds leached out
by pans of heated coals
everyone bidding each other good morning
supping at the dining table together, conversing
and though no cowshed in the backyard
there might be a hen or two for fresh eggs daily
which I have succumbed to eating
to keep up and refresh my strength
this is how it ought to be
no matter where one lives
to look each other in the eye
and not have it deemed disrespectful
no matter what the sex, and yet—
they regard me, here, highly because of my caste
that I am some sort of royalty ensconced in silk
calling me the Hindoo woman from India
the high caste medical student of special lineage
descended of seven wise sages
appealing to their exotic leanings
oh, if only they knew—
of the ill-fated widow back home
sequestered in a dark, spare room
the sight of her face bad luck

she is a Hindoo too, biding her time
counting grains of rice, those hollow days
of her life separating husk from grain
for those tonsured priests
those holier than thou mouths
bidding her stay

away

A DRESS FOR ANNIE

Favorite Name, Male and Female—Rama, Tara, Annie, Gopal, Vishnu, and Chrishna.

—From a mental photograph of Anandibai Joshee in
Mrs. Theodocia Carpenter's Autograph book, Roselle,
New Jersey, 1883.

1883

Sometimes I wonder what might it be like
        to don a bonnet, my black hair twisted into coils

fringing my forehead, and the corset though it looks
        most uncomfortable, would define my waist more

what might be the color of the dress to go with it
        what type of ruffles and how big the bustle?

and what if they called me Annie instead of Anandi?
        Aunt tells me time and again to wear hers

though she is taller and larger than I am
        I have lifted her dress in my arms

dancing with it as if a ghost, but never
        have I worn a western dress, and if ever

it were to be, I should wear my kunku, mangalsutra and bangles
for without them, I would feel my worth forsaken

what I fear most is the ridicule, and also the thought
that I might actually like it, and then what will I tell him—

he whose letters arrive from thousands of miles away
informing me I have changed, though he is not my witness

THEY CALL ME LADY OF THE ORIENT

Philadelphia, September 1883

Though the darkest one in the room, I'm the brightest of them all
in a red Pitambar saree deemed Pompeiian, belle of this ball—
and as I shake their hands, five hundred pairs, wearing gloves
to protect me, they regard the spray of pearls hanging
from my nose, my filigreed wrists of bangles glinting gold
the tiny kunku dot on my broad forehead drawing stares
and praise, for this young Hindoo lady so brave, having come
all the way alone from Serampore to the city of brotherly love
to earn her doctor's coat. *Majhe nav Anandi aahe*, I want to say
in my native tongue, so that I don't forget who I am
the young girl whose books once lay tattered in the cowshed
whose baby lived barely ten days—I float like an Indian rose
among a dull sea of cinched waists and bonnets, in the parlor
of the Dean of the Women's Medical College, smiling
till my cheeks hurt as they stumble out a new version of
my name, Ananda Bye, remarking how exquisite is my English

WHEN THE GUESTS SUP AS GODS: A GHAZAL

Roselle, New Jersey, 1883

In my wildest dreams, never do I fathom tonight
that I should turn them into feasting Indians tonight

not those whose vast plains they call their own
but proud Mahrattas from my faraway native tonight

all the fair ladies draped in woven bordered sarees
hands bangled, necks spangled, shining bright tonight

as they swish across the inlaid floor like princesses
in my colorful trousseau that belongs to them tonight

eighteen squares hand-drawn in red and white powder
on the dining room floor where guests sup as Gods tonight

set with plates stitched from broad buttonwood leaves
a rich meal of spiced vegetables and fruit await all tonight

after a Sanskrit prayer blessing this feast is chanted
all eyes look up to me on how to proceed tonight

no spoons, no forks, nor knives, just their pale bare hands
sampling eighteen exotic dishes prepared by myself tonight

fashioning small balls out of their food with pink fingertips
they pop them into their mouths like all of India does tonight

the meal ends with a serenade and sprinkling of rosewater
bouquets of freshly plucked flowers given to each guest tonight

Oh Anandi, see the red kunku on all their white foreheads
how the love of my new sisters makes this heart swell tonight

A DISTINGUISHED BRAHMIN LADY VISITS TIFFANY & COMPANY

New York City, 1883

With a lurch and clop of the horsecar, we are off to take in the sights of the city, its hustle and bustle stirring my heart, reminding me of home. We are riding through the Ladies Mile at Union Square, New York, and everywhere my eyes rest—women dressed so fine, their bonnets bobbing and corsets cinched tight. This is where the American gentry come to purchase garments and sundry and window-shop at stores like Lord & Taylor, Siegel-Cooper, and Macy's. I am a speck among these massive multistory buildings of iron, glass, and stone. The Prince of Wales once stayed here on 5th Avenue, Aunt tells me, before we alight at 15th, the tentacles of empire so far reaching, when suddenly we halt in front of a giant statue of Atlas almost naked, greeting us with a clock in his hands instead of the earth. We are at the entrance of Tiffany and Company—a *modern palace of jewels*, telling all who pass it by, we have all the time in the world.

Inside, behind dark walnut wood counters, there is a swish of activity—formalities are exchanged as they ascertain our purpose. Aunt introduces me as the distinguished Brahmin lady who is studying medicine to uplift the women of her nation and they usher us in like royalty. I let her words slide off my shoulders, remembering how when I left, my countrymen deemed me a traitor for desiring to cross black waters. My brooch of rubies and pearls catches the jeweler's eye, as does my emerald and gold bracelet, my saree of silk pinned to the side, they remark most elegant. And after much admiration, they ask me to regard the treasures they have, displayed in endless ebony cases—silver teapots, opera glasses, and pale gold watches of the wrist and pocket, 18 carats. We discuss the purity of gold and precious stones, how Burma has the best rubies, when they bring out their possession most prized, encased in satin, the Tiffany yellow diamond, found in the colonies of Southern Africa. I think of how far it has traveled, how it was rough when they first found it; its brilliance revealed after being polished—82 extraordinary facets— and feel a strange kinship with this object, the subject of so many eyes. We leave after a few hours without making a purchase, where time stilled as we feasted on such opulent treasures, feeling the fullness of a thousand meals consumed, without our lips having touched a silver spoon.

LOVE ACROSS BLACK WATERS

.I.

April-June, 1883

My heart sank as I left you in the company of strangers

I hoped to enjoy the sea without satiety

The City of Calcutta took you away and left me stranded

but soon my eyes grew weary

watching your body become a speck as if a bird in the sky

seasick and homesick on this floating island

I feared the ocean's waters might hypnotize you

my repose disturbed a hundred times

and is any place a home without us together?

this separation from you is most unbearable

And I wonder if they've fed you well

well-nigh on the point of starvation

not succumbing to animal flesh

my few potatoes to their long-boned meats

the nights stretch long and silent

I seek comfort in my companion most quiet

the opening of a new book

pages filled with words that do not judge me

.II.

Summer, 1883

Such joy I feel on receiving your letters

I hope you draw courage from my weekly missives

each envelope carrying clods of home

(and) the red earth that once clung to your feet

hands tracing the slant of your words

keep strong as you buoy the hopes of a nation

let not others discourage you

shine the eye of your kunku on all

I will remain myself as I bring change

having crossed such turbulent black waters

for the women of my land so deserving

putting the needs of others before one's own

of good health and compassion

as India's daughter become India's doctor

they treat me like their own here

on western shores

yet adopt our ways too

I light a lamp in front of our deities

hands folded each morning in a namaste

may victory always be yours

we greet the god within one another

.III.

Fall, 1883

What I was afraid of has happened

my integrity greatly measured from such a long distance

all I taught you undone like a knot

under your able guidance I thrive in this new land

style of saree altered, and what next?

I never tire of upholding my native

Will the next photograph be of you in Western dress?

all during the day a saree draped on my person

What if I fail to recognize you

make no mistake as to how they see me

breath scented with animal flesh

though you said to adjust if necessary

enjoying their American ways

I refuse their food as they readily eat mine

relishing the other till it is no longer

aunt claiming we are becoming Hindoo by the day

perhaps even a change of name

as they don my sarees and kunku

forsaking well-worn traditions

Eighmie answering to Premala, Aunt to Mavshi

my eyes bearing witness

I remain your Anandi across black waters

SCORCHED RICE & COCKERELS

Women's Medical College, Philadelphia, October 1883

Yesterday the rice was undercooked and today I almost burned it,
smoke filling my room like a ghost. I was so tired and hungry, I ate
it without remorse. I am getting used to being my own mistress,
attending to my own will. The classes are rigorous, but not difficult.
Every free moment I get, apart from the daily routine of toilette, cooking,
and correspondence, my face is pressed to my books, the day's learnings.
Though I feel lonely at times, I am accompanied by the ticking
of this alarm clock which Carpenter Uncle bought me before leaving
Roselle. I have never seen anything quite like it—Five inches tall, almost
four inches wide. On one side, a small bowl like the ones we serve
ghee in our native which houses the alarm bell. On setting the hour
and then winding the hand, the clock rings sharp and shrill at the
appointed time. It rouses me each morning as if a mechanical cockerel.

UNDER THEIR VEIL OF KINDNESS

In every corner of this country, kindness
they love me so dearly here
I do not feel alone or far from home
the children greet me politely
the laundress charges me less
and the dean of the medical college
her heart so large, she gives me a place
at her hearth, when she sees I am but a mess
trying to cook then rush for classes
how to ever repay such a debt
their generosity as big as their country
and I am stubborn
In what I eat and how I dress
lentils and rice for all meals
with the occasional egg
my kunku, my bangles, my saree
I don throughout all seasons
wrapping it in such a fashion
that no cold may seep in
I like this bit of difference in which
they regard me, praise my foreignness
how in me they see my motherland
and yet their remarks like leaves
fallen on a lake, sometimes float with ignorance
Do your homes in India have windows?

How do you see God in stone?
Why are your brides so young?
Are there many women where you come from?
To them, we are smug in our heathenness
the missionaries who come back
echoing the same, and so it is up to me
to pierce through their many veils

EBONY, IVORY & SILK

1884

Over my doctor's white coat
and the black-beaded mangalsutra
that lays snugly against my chest
as proof of marriage—
tips of ivory in each ear
connected by tubes wrapped in fine silk
forming a parabola, a conduit of sound
from which hangs an ebony medallion
confirming proof of life through the steady gallop
of beating heart and burbling lungs

And I wonder how this is not considered
a type of precious jewelry as well
the stethoscope worn by a rare few of my sex

MESSAGE IN A BOTTLE

Philadelphia, January 1884

How dazzling the snow
dappled with sun
its light filling my eyes
as if a thousand diamonds winking
if I could bottle it up
and send it to you, oh, how I would!
So cold is it here, all the branches bare
covered in ice so clear as if framed in glass
So busy are we, like worker bees,
from 9 to 9, morning to night
doctors in training, we go to college
when it is light, but return by
the glow of the moon
and someone slips, always
on the roads that are smooth
as a mirror, most often those
who have not worn rubber boots
for fear of their legs looking fat
but I am not one of them so vain
I trudge happily in the snow
a union suit under my saree
shawl wrapped around my head
imagining you by my side, warm

and cozy, though this cold and damp
I dare not wish on you, used to tropical
climes, yet snow is that teacher most divine
falling softly without much fanfare
covering big and small, short and tall
embracing all in its blanket of white

DISSECTION: A PANTOUM

Women's Medical College of Pennsylvania, 1884

Were it not an infant, how much easier it would be
only two of us in the room, the others having turned away
that hours ago, he might have suckled at her breast
how still the dissection table under our studious gaze

Only two of us in the room, the others having turned away
a pale boy with wisps of blond hair, curled fists, blue lips
how still the dissection table under our studious gaze
aborted or succumbed to illness, is what we must ascertain

A pale boy with wisps of blond hair, curled fists, blue lips
unlike my own, dark with a thick shock of hair
aborted or succumbed to illness, is what we must ascertain
I am surprised when my hand glides, how it doesn't shake

Unlike my own, dark with a thick shock of hair
his loss accepted without inquiry or investigation
I am surprised when my hand glides, how it doesn't shake
making a *vertical incision from the skin before backward*

His loss accepted without inquiry or investigation
I have not traveled this far to let history repeat itself
making a *vertical incision from the skin before backward*
I search for the answers I myself did not get

I have not traveled this far to let history repeat itself
were it not an infant, how much easier it would be
I search for the answers I myself did not get
that hours ago, he might have suckled at her breast

A SCALPEL IN HER BONNET

"We consider the needle a much more appropriate weapon in the hands of a woman than the scalpel or bistoury.
—Fanny Fern, columnist/humorist, editorial, Boston Review, 1855

She doctor
beardless non-blusher
sexless being
doctoress
no matter which continent we inhabit
synonyms arise
of what they can't comprehend
a woman with a scalpel and so they protest
I shan't submit my pulse to anything that wears a bonnet!
Though a body unconscious knows not the sex
of the hand that secures the suture, makes the cut

MENAGERIE: AN ABECEDARIAN POEM

Barnum & Bailey Circus, Philadelphia 1884

America is great for many things
But certainly not this—inside the hippodrome
Crowds 5000 strong, and I, just one face
Dromedaries racing with Nubians riding
Elephants parading in the streets
Fancies of the Orient most savage and exotic
Grand the lions in a ring, heeding a cracked whip
How dare they think I should feel at home
In seeing the Indian midget, hobbling to and fro
Jesting for their pleasure with his miniature limbs
Knife thrower, I beg, aim at my heart, and still this pain I feel
Laugh as they do at these antics, yet stoic I remain
Menagerie of humans, who conceives of such a thing?
No pleasure whatsoever, do I derive from any of this
Of oddities and ethnicities considered uncivilized
Public humiliation in the guise of entertaining
Question, yes, I do, if I'm regarded as the same
Recollecting how they stroked my hair, caressed my skin
Showing their affection is what my naive heart believed
Till this circus opened my eyes and filled them to the brim
Uncivilized is the culture that mocks other ones, and
Verily I believe it will be this nation's downfall

When one race passes judgment on another
Xenophobia masked as the Greatest Show on Earth
Yes, Americans surely know how to please a crowd
Zealously they drag all of humanity down

A VISIT TO THE SPRINGS

1884, Saratoga, New York

I will not let my pain interfere with anybody's happiness, not even my own. My body, still used to the tropics, unable to adjust, aches with every movement. And this headache, which is my constant companion, I ignore as we make our way through the countryside. In Troy, I try cucumber pickles that are unusually green. No one can tell me why and I suspect they have copper in them. When I run a needle through a pickle, it turns bright red and then I am satisfied. Someone remarks how that is my doctor's mind. In Saratoga, the women roam freely without their bonnets, and their hair like fine silk, flutters in the summer breeze as they visit the springs. I find out this is the land of the Iroqouis tribe. I meet a squaw and we exchange notes on how different our Indianness is. As we part, she gives me a necklace of beads and calls me sister. I give her a copper ¼ anna coin with Empress Victoria on one side.

WHEN THEY ASK US TO POSE FOR A PHOTOGRAPH AT THE WOMEN'S MEDICAL COLLEGE RECEPTION

Philadelphia, 1885

Forgive us if we don't smile
the ocean's scent still on our clothes

still on our clothes the stench of sea
we, visitors of another clime

of warmer lands are we
with pride, we wear our native clothes

silks and jewels we proudly don
saree, kimono, headdress of coins

with lyre, sash, a handheld fan
no scalpel, stethoscope or degree

three female doctors of foreign pedigree
playing dress-up for Western eyes

in our appearance, they see worlds wild
forgive us if we don't smile

SOON WE WILL BE REUNITED

On GopalRao's arrival in the United States

1885

Three years gone and all I can think of is how we will greet each other, my dreams of our togetherness so vivid and here they are fond of kissing on the cheek. Will you mind if I do so in public, or on meeting do we shake hands like friends? I don't want you to think me shameless, though I am all the same parts, you will find me changed—still your beloved Anandi but more grown, my English so fluent and rapid, they almost think me American born. And yes, my Marathi is a little rusty, but it will always be my first tongue, I grow weary waiting, why must you make me the last stop? Speeches in so many cities, of how our culture is the grandest one. And they are too polite to call you arrogant upfront, though the news drifts to our ears. Oh, please be mindful of the kindness that this wife of yours continues to bear. You worry that all my attention will be on my studies, but rest assured every night my last thought is of you before the body commands sleep, and on waking my every action in your shadow, as I eagerly await your form.

BRACELET OF GOLD

Philadelphia, 1886

Some would say this a bad omen, buri nazar
penance for crossing waters dark as kohl
to live alone among people white as snow
Still unused to these harsh northeast winters
I miss the patch of ice that shines like a mirror
and my right-hand lands first to brace the fall
Though no bones are broken, all my bangles shatter
in the manner of a Hindoo widow, bits of green glass
pressing into my skin, drawing out the red

When my husband finds my wrist
unadorned, lacking any ornamentation
he slides into place a bracelet of gold
cold like the touch of his fingers
and *if every fall would bring as much gold*
would you consider it a misfortune?
I call it so, wishing instead an instrument
more useful or a book more instructive

THESIS

Ink spills in a mannerly fashion
fifty pages written near the hearth's fire
of knowledge so natural, it seems almost redundant
passed through wombs centuries over, wisdom
from my ancestors that men guard like jewels
I lay claim on it now, without apologies
childbirth among my kind, this universal experience
which women know so intimately, yet shy away
from complaints and concerns at the hands
of the other sex who simply can't know it
for male bodies merely offer seed
neither soil nor plant can they possess
—and a quickening of pulse will detect it
a line of divine writing, pregnancy's radius
stretching from the pubes to the umbilical
cessation of the monthly red
'little nipples' rising on the breast
nausea, fatigue, thirst
diagnosis through the five senses
a poultice of mustard seeds for excess emesis
hips raised toward the sky
to prevent abortion of the fetus
for three years I took their generous learnings
women doctors of the West, and now I offer them mine
Obstetrics Among the Aryan Hindoos
no matter how heathen or civilized, they will see
birth is that great unifier in the way we all emerge

AN INVITATION TO PRACTICE

March 1886

The Dewan writes to Dr. Bodley
on hearing of my impending qualification
nothing could be more desirable
than to have a native of India for our doctor
my designation, Lady Doctor of Kolhapur
Oh, how fate manages to come full circle
in the very city where this very dream began!
Rs. 300 my starting salary, to increase
over the years, my passage to India
to be borne by the state, as long as
I remain in service for more than one
though they want me for seven, to take
charge of Edward Albert hospital
I see myself striding its gothic halls
my saree swishing against the stone floors
as I administer to my own people
under guidance of the Durbar doctor
and so I make haste to accept the offer
where they will give me a house
with ordinary furniture, a class of girls
to instruct in medicine, future practitioners
my only caveat, to never charge a fee
from those poor and depressed

COMMENCEMENT

At noon, on the llth of March, I went to the Green Room of the Academy of Music, where the Graduation Exercises were to be held. It was full of bright young girls and flowers. When we went out upon the stage, we confronted an audience of three thousand persons.
—Mrs. Caroline Dall, on Anandibai Joshee's graduation ceremony from The Women's Medical College of Pennsylvania

June 11, 1886, Philadelphia

We are bright young girls with flowers
first flush of roses blooming
dressed in our finest garments
sweeping the stage like sea foam
amidst claps so thunderous
it rattles the beams, 33 women
under oath to *do good or to do no harm*
primum non nocere, destined
to treat and heal, to soothe
ailments small and big, our touch
sorely needed where only men have gone
not a tremble on my lip, but my heart beating
loud as the clop of a streetcar horse
people as far as the eye can see
upon the steps, aisles, and walls
all look at me, all look at me
my loved and those beloved
whose presence is gift enough
smiling as they announce my name

ascending the dais to claim my degree
eyes moist with pride, *so much that comes after*
than goes before, I almost break down and cry
my patience worn down to a thread
my body frail as a kite, my exams finished
on fumes of resolve, I passed, and now here I am
clad in white silk and gold, and though
they call me brave, announce my name,
the prefix of doctor before it, I am astonished
at how this feat was done, this title
on which I now lay claim

A COMMENDATION FROM THE QUEEN

July 14, 1886

The dean, Dr. Bodley, is giddy with joy
in her hands, a letter from the Queen
that she waves in front of my eyes
—Empress Victoria, whose men continue
to plunder our land, the Koh-i-noor snug
against her chest shining bright, commanded
her secretary to reply how *she read the news
of my graduation with great interest*—and that
I should be all smiles, my success spread far & wide

HANDS

Summer, 1886

Aai,

It is as if the cold has entered my bones and refuses to go. I long for a hot meal prepared by your hands. Only then will I recover. I dream of that day when before me lies a thali of varan-bhat, bhaji and bhakri, to scoop it up with my hands, no spoon, no fork, just fingertips to lips. American people do not know of that joy though I have tried to teach them. Here, the food is unworthy. It is without spice and goes down the throat like sand. And just how do they manage to half cook rice even when it is steeped in water? I realize, now the simple pleasures of what we all take for granted, that Sanskrit utterance before we eat, annadata sukhibhava, may the provider of this food be happy.

OF RED

Delaware County, NY, 1886

How bright the stain
of strawberries
on our tongues and lips
we pluck and *eat the fruit*
heartily
seedy hearts I hold
in moist palms
this greed to consume them all
and in its sugar
I lose myself
its tinge of sour
bursting
like fireworks
basket in hand
Eighmie and I trail its patches
her skirt and my saree swishing
through long rows of green
punctured by pulsing red
and though *I have not botanized*
I inhale fresh country air
they promise will do me good
Oh, let these berries be my cure!
We roam about and work

my chest straining and yet
I put aside shivers, coughs
a throat inflamed
—at the hospital, I minister
a difficult birth, ten hours
before we hear the coveted cry
at home, my *crazy work*
a distraction from
the heaviness in my lungs
a quilt of many hues a different kind
of patch, I lose myself
in fabric scraps
from cherished friends
tonight, I choose a berry
block to sew, every stitch
tart and sweet

OUR HEARTS, A THOUSAND HORSES

Carlisle, Pennsylvania, 1886

How to describe the feeling
of being stripped naked while fully clothed
a spectator to erasure, the bile rising as we stop
in the town of Carlisle, at an Indian boarding school
on invitation by Captain Pratt, its founder, as he shows off
the former army barracks now deemed a place of learning
his pride a contrast of boys and girls who once donned tribal finery
now dressed in Western clothes, *Kill the Indian, Save the Man,* his motto
we are told, and as the captain bids me to assess their health,
I think of how I have held steadfast to my apparel, my food,
my spiritual views, not forced to adapt in these three years,
though certainly encouraged for the greater good,
as they bid me good morning and good day, children
whose mother tongues and birth names have been obliterated
whose skin shade I share, along with a race misattributed
I look into their eyes, shining, peer down their throats, pink
listen to their hearts that gallop strong as a thousand horses, and think
how all hearts sound the same regardless of intentions
after a talk on personal hygiene, amidst claps of appreciation
when I am asked what I think of my visit, I remark most illuminating

CRAZY (QUILT) WORK

New York, July 1886

Resourcefulness knows no nationality
among women tending the hearth—
we are mistresses of improvisation
magicians of the ordinary
those fabric scraps whose warp
and weft seem exhausted, we collect
like leaves till they are plenty
a motley come together haphazardly
no symmetry, no intentional design
just hardworking fingers patching
together what seems out of order
this *crazy work*, an American pastime
becomes this Mahratta woman's way
to pass a summer filled with anticipation
and premonition, so much to be done
so little the time to do it, these gifted
blocks of cloth, beating bright with
love and generosity, become a quilt
that covers my *unseasonal chills*, my
malaise for which no cure fits

RETURN TO THE MOTHERLAND

October 1886, New York

The past month spent in Aunt's home
whose every crevice I have come to love
and think my own, from bed to lounge
to dining room, I lose myself in conversation
these last dregs of merriment, between chills
and fever, till the morning of our departure arrives
eleven trunks packed by she, who I consider
a mother, eight of them purely souvenirs
white and blue pottery mottled by salt
and the crazy quilt, each block of fabric
bearing the heart of a precious friend. There can be
no other like her, my dearest Aunt Carpenter
who all these years expected nothing in return
except for my well-being, and how does one say
goodbye to one's most treasured of humans
If only there were a way to stay with her forever
I cough with each turn of my pen
even the least breeze seems to abuse me
my strength so reduced, I cling to the carriage
as we make our way to the port, stopping briefly
at all the homes that opened their doors to me
once we set sail I grasp onto each breath
as if at the ship's taffrail, steadying myself
for the journey back, a native's return
a gloam of goodbyes
lingering   over my head

A HUNGER FOR HOME

Aboard the HMS Etruria & P. and O. Company's steamer Peshawar, 1886

How the sea shakes us so
a storm in these waters
tossing us from our beds
downing the strongest of brandies
I try to still this wicked cough
that rises like a tide gone wild
and tears run unbidden
like the rain outside
my time has come, I tell him
who ministers to me day and night
my husband now my servant
instead of the other way around
one day I am silver, the next day gold
most brittle of leaves clinging to a branch
in bed all day with poultices, writing
while lying down, whenever I have the strength
and the ship's doctor visits twice a day
the twinkle in my eye shrinking
my vigor fading, as I miss my precious aunt
the crackers she gave me consumed, no food
worthy of this non-meat-eater, as they offer me beef tea
we change ships in London & they hold us back
no space for Hindoos, as Christians sail to our land

when we finally get a first-class berth, it is only for one
my husband curls up on deck braving the elements
my fevered dreams of what I will eat when I reach home
the ocean endless, my breaths measured, as I wonder
what will be stilled first, the waters or me

ON ARRIVAL

.I.

He bids all European medicines be stopped
to let nature take its course
after the ship's surgeon prescribed
champagne, brandy, claret & whiskey
with little success, as I decried stimulants
and homeland air will surely be the cure
my husband promises this ailing doctor
who fails to heal herself
and as we touch Bombay's harbor
I don a black nauvari saree, around the waist
through my legs, with a khun blouse
shoes and thick stockings that shield me
from the cool November air, my nose ring
glinting as I step out in the Indian sun
that comes at us in thick slants
its heat permeating every pore
as they row us to shore, a shower
of flowers and faces that greet us
as foot touches floor
matrabhumi, motherland
that first breath drawn on arrival
mi ghari aahe, I am home, I am whole

.II.

They call us *plucky*, a *noble example*
of moral courage & *perseverance*
the ink of newspapers spreading
word of India's first female doctor
on arrival from America, and those
that doubted my qualifications
now speak sweet words of praise
fill our home night and day
with salutations and felicitations
gifts of flowers, money, pens
this heroic act of samudra langhan
becomes a worthy husband's doing
his *aim achieved*, his *determination*
to give his wife a useful education
my courage and hard work borne
from *deferential obedience*
to his command, but those who know me
know this is not quite so, the truth always
more complicated, but instead of denial
I focus at the task at hand, how to
recover amidst the din of admiration
my hospital ward awaiting
this new doctor's sure stride
one day I am bright & lively
the next day fevered
and they wonder whose nazar
is upon me, when it will abate

.III.

Home, yet not at home
we remove from house to house
one unfurnished, the other damp
and yet have I to eat a meal
after my mother's fashion
three weeks in and they conclude
it is consumption that plagues me
the dry of hills prescribed, and so
we rush to Pune, land of my birth
cool breezes greeting us on arrival
my body so much reduced, they think me
a child, yet my spirits buoyed
dreams cloaked in my doctor's coat
as they give me native medicine
spoons of hope that first still my cough
then recall it, mother finally feeds me all
my heart desires, bakhri crushed with her fingers
and in my dreams, I roam hospital halls
examining patient after patient
when suddenly they charge in, missionary ladies
slapping bibles into the hands of the ailing
I wake up bathed in sweat, my body shaking
Aai at my side, wiping my forehead
gentle unlike the way when I was young
it is never too late for affection
it is never too soon for love

THE END

February 26, 1887

I have done all that I could
so much surmounted
but for death, & I go surrounded
by love, my obligations shed
consumed by fire
ashes returned to earth
I leave you with embers
to fan as you wish

oh mother

oh mother

oh mother

We gave her a religious fire. There was a goodly crowd. People had no notice nor could we keep the body longer. That warmness vanished and the body became cold and changed. I now understand why death is said to be cold.

—Gopalrao, in a letter to Theodocia Carpenter

Alas, what sorrow is ours, who knew and loved her? The inevitable is upon us, and with a fate in God who doeth all things well, let us bear this dispensation with hearts turned toward Him, believing that there is some wise providence in the early departure of this noble soul.

—attributed to Mrs. Theodocia Carpenter

Anandibai Joshee was cremated in India following full Hindu rites that included a mourning period of thirteen days. Amidst much protest and criticism, Anandibai's husband, Gopalrao, sent her ashes to Theodocia Carpenter in America, as a gesture to honor the love Anandibai had for America and her aunt whom she considered a second mother. Anandibai's ashes rest in Poughkeepsie, New York's Rural Cemetery amidst the Eighmie-Carpenter family. Her gravestone reads:

ANANDABAI
JOSHEE M.D.
1865—1887
FIRST BRAHMIN WOMAN
TO LEAVE INDIA TO OBTAIN
AN EDUCATION

GLOSSARY

Aai (Marathi)-Mother. P. 12, 13, 14, 16, 22, 77, 84.

Jhopala (Marathi): Traditional Indian wooden swing suspended from the ceiling by brass chains. P. 11, 13, 16, 23

Malla (Sanskrit): Wrestler. P. 14

Zenana (Hindi/Urdu): Women's quarters. P. 14, 17, 44

Mardana (Hindi/Urdu): Men's quarters. P. 14

Pakshala (Marathi): Kitchen. P. 16

Gaud (Marathi): Jaggery. P. 17, 20

Ashtakoot (Sanskrit): Eight aspects of Vedic astrology used to determine marriage compatibility. P. 18

Bhinn shahere (Marathi): Different cities. P. 18

Tujhe nav kahe (Marathi): What is your name. P. 18

Majhe nav Yamuna Gunpatrao Joshee aahe (Marathi): My name is Yamuna Gunpatrao Joshee. P. 18, 56

Phulapakhare (Marathi): Butterflies. P. 19

Lapachhapi (Marathi): Hide-n-seek. P. 19

Nauvari: Traditional Maharashtrian nine-yard saree worn on auspicious occasions. P. 19, 22, 83

Mandav (Marathi): Wedding pavilion. P. 19, 20

Antarpat: Cloth held between bride and groom, which on lowering signifies two souls becoming one. P. 19, 20

Doke, khanda, ghudga, payachi botey (Marathi): Head, shoulders, knees, toes. P. 23

Kunku (Marathi): Bindi/Kumkum. P. 23, 29, 49, 55, 56, 57, 61, 63.

Bhandi-kundi (Marathi): Pots and pans. P. 31

NOTES

Facts, incidents and extracts from Anandibai's letters are mostly culled from two primary texts, *The Life of Dr Anandabai Joshee: A Kinswoman of the Pundita Ramabai* by Caroline Healey Dall and *A Fragmented Feminism: The Life and Letters of Anandibai Joshee* by Meera Kosambi. Where there is a direct reference or quote in the poem, I have marked this by the author's last name followed by the corresponding page number.

"A Different Kind of Arithmetic": Dall, 22-23.

"Mark & Mar": Kosambi, 17-18.

"Riding with Miss Moysey": Kosambi, 21. Moysey is misspelt as Micey in Kosambi's book.

"Saraswati in My Satchel": Dall, 85.

"My Husband Writes a Letter to Reverend Wilder": Italicized lines from *The Missionary Review*, 1879, pp 49-50, Dall 3.

"The Whole Universe is a Lesson to Me: Epistolary Exchanges": Dall, 35-78. Kosambi, 31-59.

"Why I Go to America": Dall, 82-91. Kosambi, 91-93.

"Riding the Meridian": Dall, 94-95. Kosambi, 100-103.

"American Lady Friends Greet a Mahratta Woman": Kosambi, 106.

"A Mental Photograph": Dall, 19-20. Kosambi, 116.

"If It Please God": Dall, 35. Kosambi, 29.

"A Plea to Make Herstory": Kosambi, 123.

"They Call Me Lady of the Orient": Kosambi, 156.

"When the Guests Sup as Gods: A Ghazal": Dall, 97-100. Kosambi, 109-110.

"A Distinguished Brahmin Lady Visits Tiffany & Company": Dall, 96.

"Love Across Black Waters": Kosambi, 107-108.

"Scorched Rice & Cockerels": Kosambi, 130.

"Under Their Veil of Kindness": Kosambi, 133.

"Message in a Bottle": Dall, 109. Kosambi, 139-142.

"Menagerie: An Abecedarian Poem": Dall, 109. Kosambi, 162.

"A Visit to the Springs": Dall, 110-111. Kosambi, 162.

"When They Ask Us To Pose...": An ekphrastic poem based on an iconic photograph of Anandibai Joshee with two other medical students from Japan and Syria.

"Bracelet of Gold": Dall, 126. Kosambi 186.

"Dissection: A Pantoum" Italicized lines from *Gray's Anatomy, 1901.* Dall, 100.

"An Invitation to Practice": Dall, 143. Kosambi, 187.

"Commencement": 131, Dall. Kosambi, 195.

"A Commendation from the Queen": Dall, 164. Kosambi, 195.

"Of Red": Dall, 161. Kosambi, 200.

"Our Hearts, A Thousand Horses": Dall, 167. Kosambi, 206.

"Crazy (Quilt) Work": Dall, 162-163. Kosambi, 200.

"Return to the Motherland": Dall, 169-171. Kosambi, 206-207.

"A Hunger for Home": Dall, 213-216. Kosambi, 176-178.

"On Arrival": Dall, 179-184. Kosambi, 218.

"The End": Dall, 184-186. Kosambi, 228.

ACKNOWLEDGEMENTS

Thanks to the editors of the following publications where these poems first appeared, sometimes in different form.

Catamaran: "To Touch the Sky"

Commonplace, The Journal of Early American Life: "They Call Me Lady of the Orient," "A Mental Photograph," "A Dress for Annie," "When the Guests Sup as Gods: A Ghazal," "A Distinguished Brahmin Lady Visits Tiffany & Company," "Scorched Rice & Cockerels," "Ebony, Ivory & Silk," "Bracelet of Gold," "Crazy (Quilt) Work"

Mom Egg Review: "Naming/Nāmkaran"

Pithead Chapel: "Outside the Chaukat," "A Visit to the Springs"

The Punch Magazine: "A Different Kind of Arithmetic," "Lagnaachi Bedi (A Suitable Match)," "Loss: An Invocation," "A Plea to Make Herstory," "Dissection: A Pantoum"

The Yearbook of Indian Poetry, 2021: "When the Guests Sup as Gods: A Ghazal"

Innumerable people have walked this path with me, helping bring *Anandibai Joshee: A Life in Poems* out into the world. To all of you who encouraged, supported, and championed this book, I echo the words and sentiments of Anandibai Joshee: *my gratitude knows no bounds.*

Thank you, Kanishka Gupta, stellar agent and friend, for always keeping it real and taking a chance on this unusual collection of poems.

HarperCollins India has been a dream to work with. My thanks to Udayan Mitra, Rahul Soni, and my editor, Prerna Gill, who has been a fount of patience as we sorted out line breaks and spacing issues. Special thanks to Sohini Basak, my commissioning editor, for deeply resonating with the vision of this project and holding it with such care.

Devangana Dash, I thank you for adorning this book with such a radiant cover.

I'm grateful to Tishani Doshi and Arundhathi Subramaniam for their artistry and commitment to women's voices and for lending their supportive words toward this endeavor.

Rajiv Mohabir, in our friendship I find community, and in your words, sunlight. Your support truly lifts me.

Soniah Kamal, brilliant wordsmith, and sister from another mother, for reading every possible version of every poem and buoying me with hope when I faltered, and for being brutally honest when needed—what can I say except that our friendship resides beyond the realm of thanks.

Other friends who have offered advice during the writing of this book and cheered me on are Urvashi Bahuguna, Chaitali Sen, Manisha Sharma, and Maw Shein Win.

Gratitude to Priya Das and Usha Srinivasan of Mosaic America, for inviting me into their extraordinary arts organization as a Mosaic fellow, supporting my work, and featuring poems from *Anandibai Joshee: A Life in Poems* in the following programs: Galorious, International Women's Day radio program featured on KPFA, 94.1 FM, 2021; San Jose Museum of Art's Third Thursdays at SJMA, Then is Still Now, 2021; Her Story in Verse, San Jose Women's Club, 2022.

Thanks, also, to Lisa Rosenberg, San Mateo County Poet Laureate Emerita, and to Monica Korde, Belmont Poet Laureate, for featuring this project in their programs.

Namrita Yuhanna, thanks for featuring this project on Off the Cuff with Namrita, 92.3 FM.

To my literary community in India, especially Lakshmi Sankar and the Bengaluru Poetry Festival, thank you for sustaining the connection over years and miles.

For translation help in Marathi, dhanyavad to Reeta Dighe and Kalyani Deshpande.

I'm indebted to the following writing communities—Shuffle Collective, South Bay Writer's Group, and the Writers Grotto—for providing nurturing creative spaces as well as camaraderie and knowledge.

So much love to my family for giving me the space to 'dwell in possibility.' Anything else I say will not be enough.

This book is for all the brave people who live in the margins, whose stories wait to be unearthed, who chart their own course and don't take no for an answer. This book is for YOU.

SELECTED REFERENCES

ARCHIVES

Drexel University Legacy Center Archives & Special Collections
South Asian American Digital Archive (SAADA)

ARTICLES

Gurjarpadhye, Prachi. "Through a Changing Feminist Lens: Three Biographies of Anandibai Joshi." *Economic and Political Weekly* (2014): 37-40.

Kosambi, Meera. "Anandibai Joshee: Retrieving a fragmented feminist image." *Economic and Political Weekly* (1996): 3189-3197.

Kosambi, Meera. "A Prismatic Presence: the Multiple Iconisation of Dr Anandibai Joshee and the Politics of Life-Writing." *Australian Feminist Studies* 16.35 (2001): 157-173.

Shetty, Sandhya. "Anandibai Joshi's Passage to America (and More): The Making of a Hindu Lady Doctor." *New Directions in Literature and Medicine Studies*, 2017, pp. 281–303

BOOKS

Dall, Caroline Wells Healey. *The Life of Dr Anandabai Joshee: A Kinswoman of the Pundita Ramabai*. Boston: Roberts Brothers, 1888.

Godbole, Rohini, and Ram Ramaswamy. *Lilavati's Daughters: The Women Scientists of India*. Indian Academy of Sciences, 2010.

Joshi, Shrikrishna Janardan, author. *Anandi Gopal.* Translated by Anjali Damle. Calcutta: Stree, 1992

Kosambi, Meera, et al. *A Fragmented Feminism: The Life and Letters of*

Anandibai Joshee. India: Routledge, 2020.

Patwardhan, Nandini. *Radical Spirits: India's First Woman Doctor and Her American Companions.* Raleigh, NC and Singapore: Story Artisan Press, 2020

Rao, Kavitha. *Lady Doctors: The Untold Stories of India's First Women in Medicine*. India: Westland Publications, 2021

WEBSITES

Falcone, Alissa. "Remembering the Pioneering Women From One of Drexel's Legacy Medical Colleges." DrexelNow, 27 Mar. 2017, drexel.edu/now/archive/2017/March/Women-Physicians/.

Verghese, Danielle. "The Graduates." The Triangle, 22 Jan. 2016, www.thetriangle.org/snowball/the-graduates/.

"The First Female Medical College: 'Will You Accept or Reject Them.'" Doctor or Doctress? doctordoctress.org/islandora/object/islandora:1496.

ABOUT THE AUTHOR

Shikha Malaviya was born in the United Kingdom but grew up in the United States and India. Her family originally hails from Uttarakhand. Shikha's first book of poems, *Geography of Tongues*, was published to acclaim in 2014. Her poetry has been nominated for the Pushcart Prize and featured in *Catamaran, PLUME, Prairie Schooner* and other fine publications. Shikha has been a featured TEDx speaker and was selected as Poet Laureate of San Ramon, California, 2016. She is co-founder of The (Great) Indian Poetry Collective, a mentorship-model literary press and is currently a Mosaic America Fellow. Shikha graduated from the University of Minnesota with degrees in liberal studies, creative writing, and mass communications. She lives in the San Francisco Bay area with her family, where she is a poetry mentor, publisher, and workshop facilitator.

30 Years *of*

HarperCollins *Publishers* India

At HarperCollins, we believe in telling the best stories and finding the widest possible readership for our books in every format possible. We started publishing 30 years ago; a great deal has changed since then, but what has remained constant is the passion with which our authors write their books, the love with which readers receive them, and the sheer joy and excitement that we as publishers feel in being a part of the publishing process.

Over the years, we've had the pleasure of publishing some of the finest writing from the subcontinent and around the world, and some of the biggest bestsellers in India's publishing history. Our books and authors have won a phenomenal range of awards, and we ourselves have been named Publisher of the Year the greatest number of times. But nothing has meant more to us than the fact that millions of people have read the books we published, and somewhere, a book of ours might have made a difference.

As we step into our fourth decade, we go back to that one word – a word which has been a driving force for us all these years.

Read.